THEN AND THERE SERIES

GENERAL EDITOR

MARJORIE REEVES, M.A., Ph.D.

Roman Britain

JOAN LIVERSIDGE, M.LITT., F.S.A.

Illustrated from contemporary sources by

D. STREDDER BIST

LONGMANS

LONGMANS, GREEN AND CO LTD

London and Harlow

Associated companies, branches and representatives
throughout the world

First published 1958
Third impression 1960
Sixth impression 1965
Seventh impression 1967
Eighth impression 1969

Acknowledgments

For permission to include line drawings based on copyright
sources we are indebted to the following: The National
Museum of Wales—pages 3, 7 (foot) and 13 from V. E. Nash
Williams: *The Roman Legionary Fortress at Caerleon*; Andrew
Reid & Co., Ltd.—pages 23 and 29 from J. Collingwood Bruce:
Handbook to the Roman Wall; The University of Wales Press
—pages 35 (foot) and 38 from *The Bulletin of the Board of
Celtic Studies*. In addition we wish to express our thanks to
the Directors of the British Museum and the London Museum
for their assistance in the preparation of the many drawings
based on originals in their possession.

Printed in Hong Kong by Peninsula Press Ltd.

ROMAN BRITAIN

CONTENTS

TO THE READER

THIS is a book about life in Roman Britain in the second century A.D. Unlike books about later English history we cannot say that every fact in it comes from some record written at the time because no British records of this early date survive for us to use. But there are many other methods of learning about Roman Britain as you will see if you read pages 72 to 80. Everything in this book is based on such sources.

In the same way most of the drawings are of things actually used by Romano-Britons. Some are copied from the pictures they carved on tombstones and a few show you what their buildings, now in ruins, would have looked like in the second century.

By studying such things you will come to feel at home in one 'patch' of the history of the past and really live with the group of people as they thought and worked then and there. And gradually you will be able to fill in more patches of history. Much more remains to be found out about Roman Britain and those of you who want to learn more about it should read ROMAN BRITAIN by Professor I. A. Richmond (Pelican History of England, Volume I).

THE ROMANS IN BRITAIN

We certainly do not want to be invaded and conquered today, but perhaps in the past it has been good for us to be conquered occasionally. Do you know how many times this had happened in our history? If not, perhaps you could find out.

It is a little more than two thousand years since the Romans first saw the island of Britain looming out of the sea as they sailed towards it across the Channel. They were led by the great Roman general Julius Caesar, and he was curious to see what our ancestors, the Britons, were like. He only made two quick raids, however, and then went back and wrote an account of Britain and the Britons (almost the first time anybody wrote about us!).

For nearly a hundred years more the Straits of Dover set the bounds to Roman rule. Then, in A.D. 43, the Emperor Claudius finally invaded our island with four *legions*[1] of Roman soldiers. They landed in Kent and marched inland, determined this time to conquer. Some Britons welcomed them, some fought hard against them, but bit by bit they conquered the whole of what we now call England and Wales. So Britain became part of the great Roman Empire.

How would you have liked to have been a Briton in the days when the Roman soldiers were fighting their way through your country? Probably not at all. It is never pleasant to be conquered, and you might very well have been one of the warlike Britons, like Caractacus or Boudicca, who hated the Romans. But by the time a

[1] You will find the meaning of words written like *this* in the Glossary on pages 85–90.

hundred years had passed—in the second century A.D.—things looked different. There was no more fighting now except away in the north, where the Roman soldiers kept off fierce tribes of people and so made the country safe. A Briton in the second century might be rich and comfortable and friendly with the Roman soldiers and officials who kept the land peaceful. Of course you would grumble at the heavy taxes to be paid to the Emperor, but you would probably be proud that Britain belonged to the Roman Empire and you would certainly not want the Roman soldiers to go away.

The Roman armies actually stayed in Britain for nearly four hundred years, and during that time people built many roads, forts, towns and country houses (called *villas*). Today, if you follow the clues given by maps, you can find many traces of things built by our Roman conquerors. Now they are crumbling in ruins, but once they were grand and magnificent. By using all the clues and a bit of imagination too, we can picture for ourselves how people lived in Roman Britain. Some of these people (especially the soldiers) were really foreigners from other parts of the Roman Empire, but most of them must have been Britons, now looking so like other Romans in dress and behaviour that you really could not tell them apart. So we call them Romano-British people.

SOLDIERING WITH THE SECOND LEGION

First of all we are going to look at a fortress where some of
the Roman army lived. They called it Isca Silurum: today
we know it as Caerleon, which means 'fort of the legion'.
The Second Legion was stationed at Caerleon. Here are
Gaius and Julius, two of the soldiers or *legionaries*, waiting
to greet us. They have been drilling, so they are fully
armed. Both carry *javelins* or spears in their right hands
for throwing at the enemy. Can you see the other weapons
they have ready to use after the javelins have been thrown?

3

There is a sword in the *scabbard* hanging from the shoulder strap and a dagger attached to the belt. To defend themselves against the enemy's spears and arrows, they have shields made of leather stretched over wood strengthened with a bronze *boss* in the centre, and with strips of bronze or iron binding at the edges. Julius wears a thick leather tunic and breeches; Gaius has armour in the form of pieces of metal sewn or strapped to his tunic. Both have boots made of strips of leather with thick leather soles studded with hobnails. They wear bronze helmets with sidepieces covering the ears, and a flap of metal jutting out behind to protect the back of the neck. One helmet has a ring sticking up on top of it. This is for the plume the soldier will wear on parade when the Emperor or a general comes to inspect the troops.

When we meet them Gaius and Julius are returning to the fortress after a hard day's work on the parade ground. Yesterday the news came that an important messenger from the Emperor was on his way to inspect the Second Legion. So now everyone is busy getting ready for him.

Gaius is grumbling because he is a very clever *mason* and usually spends his time building stone walls for the *barracks* and other buildings inside the fortress. Julius is getting tired of his grumbling and at last tells him to shut up. "It will do you good!" he says. "A soldier should always be practising with his weapons, and even if your back does ache, you know after the parade there will be a show in the *amphitheatre* in honour of the Emperor's messenger. We shall all enjoy that." "If Vibius Proculus goes on drilling us for hours as he did today," replies Gaius crossly, "I shall be in the hospital, and then the Legion can just wait for their new barrack building." "Cheer up, my poor friend," says Julius.

4

"What you need is a cup of wine and then you'll feel better."

Here is a picture of Vibius Proculus. Gaius and Julius belong to his *century* of eighty men—not a hundred as you might expect. He wears a metal breastplate and shoulder plates over a tunic with short sleeves and a double kilt, and he has a cloak over his shoulder. Round his waist is an elaborate belt and he is armed with sword and dagger. In his right hand is a short cane made from the branch of a vine. This vinestick is his badge of office as a centurion and he does not hesitate to use it on the backs of soldiers who are not doing their work properly. Six centuries form a *cohort*, and ten cohorts make up the legion. The first cohort is larger than the others and it is commanded by the chief centurion. He is a very important person who holds his exalted post for a year, and then either retires or receives further promotion. The Legion also includes a squadron of men on horseback about 120 strong, who were used as orderlies and despatch riders rather than as cavalry. With the officers, N.C.O.s, clerks and various odd-job men the Second Legion has a total strength of over 6,000.

As they come in sight of the gate Gaius and Julius wave to a friend who is on sentry duty, marching up and down the *rampart* walk on top of the walls. These stone walls are more than twenty feet high and surround the fortress. Then they come to the wooden bridge which crosses the ditch. You can imagine how this deep ditch with its steep sides helps to defend the fortress. It stops raiders from getting too close to the walls without warning. It makes it easier for the legionaries to hurl javelins at them as they scramble across it and try to climb the walls.

Julius and Gaius go in through the south-west gate, one of the four big gates of the fortress. Each gate has two entrances wide enough for a cart to go through, with towers on either side. They turn to the left along the road just inside the walls, then to the right, and then down a narrow street and so into their room. The barrack buildings are built back to back, facing inwards on to a common street or court, and a whole century lives in each one. The centurion and the non-commissioned officers have a block of rooms at the end nearest the fortress wall, and the legionaries are divided into twelve groups, each with an

6

inner and an outer room to share between them. If you look now at the plan of two barracks you will see how it goes:

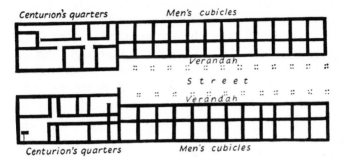

The men use the larger outer room for eating and sleeping, and they keep all their kit in the smaller room. In front of this is a verandah, the posts of which are marked by tiny squares of dots. This provides them with a covered space where they can clean their armour and mend their clothes. In this picture you see the ends of three blocks of barracks, also the wall and the ditch outside:

7

Gaius helped to build these walls and barrack buildings. He lives in the block in the foreground of our picture. The windows in the men's quarters have no glass in them, but Vibius Proculus, the centurion, has thick glass window-panes in his windows. All the rooms have tiled or cement floors. We can also see another view of the rampart walk where Julius's friend is on sentry-go, and we can look down into the deep ditch outside. At the top of the picture we notice some smoke, and if we walked past there, we should smell cooking. These are the cookhouses, placed well away from the buildings as a precaution against fire.

The legionaries lived mostly upon lard and corn made into bread or porridge, so each century had several of the big bronze bowls called camp kettles to cook it in. We do not know what happened to Vibius Proculus's

 camp kettle, but this picture shows one like it found at York, another legionary fortress. An *inscription* scratched on its side tells us that it belonged first to the century of Attilius Severus, and then the century of Aprilis had it.

No doubt Gaius also eats other things when he has the chance. There is meat, when some of the legionaries have been out hunting, and fish in the River Usk which runs past the fortress. Sometimes the legionaries club together and buy a sheep or a pig, or eggs or honey from the people living outside the fort. They also buy or grow vegetables, and there are nuts in the woods in the autumn. They have wine to drink, and this is brought to them all the way from France and Spain in the big pottery jars called *amphorae*. They were sometimes long and thin, and sometimes round and fat, as you can see in the picture.

The most important buildings are in the centre of the fortress. They face the *via principalis* (or Main Street, as we would say) which runs between the

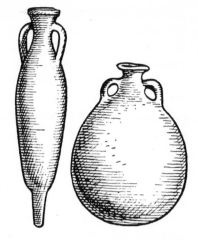

north-east and south-west gates. They include the legionary headquarters where the commanding officer, called the *Legate*, works with the staff officers. Here the army pay-chests are kept in strong-rooms under guard. The *armoury* is here, too, and the chapel for the legionary *standards*. These are the legion's dearest treasures,

prized even more than our regimental colours. The standard-bearers wear bearskin hoods over their helmets and it is their proud duty to lead the legion into battle. For a legion to lose a standard to the enemy is a terrible disgrace. Here are some splendid standards:

A standard is really a spear with a pointed end which can be stuck in the

ground, with different things at the top in place of the spearhead. One will have the Roman eagle standing on top with a *thunderbolt* in his beak. Another may have the picture of the reigning emperor. Another standard has a cross-piece of wood placed close to the top of the *shaft*, which is silver plated. Purple ribbons ending in silver ivy-leaves hang from this cross-bar, and above it is a small model shield or a wreath. Further down are bronze, saucer-shaped *discs*, the animals from the legion's badge, and symbols of good luck such as the crescent moon, or tassels or other ornaments.

The Second Legion had the title Augusta, meaning "Augustus's Own", because it was one of the legions founded by Augustus, the first Roman emperor. His birthday on September 23rd was kept as a festival by the legion. The legionary badge was the *capricorn*, an imaginary animal, half goat and half fish. Sometimes this was accompanied by the winged horse Pegasus. Here is a badge of this kind carved on a block of stone, with the shortened title LEG II AVG carved underneath. This stands for LEGIO II AUGUSTA, or Second Augustan Legion.

LEG II is also written on the standard placed between the two beasts. Properties belonging to the legion, or tiles made in the regimental *tileries*, are frequently stamped LEG II AVG.

The houses where the commandant and his officers live are near the headquarters building. So are the stables for the horses, the *granaries* with raised damp-proof floors for the corn-stores, the hospital, and the legionary prison with its rows of punishment cells. The legionaries have to learn how to build roads and forts and bridges, so there are workshops for masons, carpenters, painters, builders, *wheelwrights*, and blacksmiths, and also for *armourers*. Parties of men are sent out from the fortress to find stone for the buildings, *fodder* for the animals, and firewood, no doubt, for everybody.

Many of the supplies come up the River Usk by boat and are unloaded on the *quays* at the water's edge. A bridge crosses the river and roads from it lead in many directions. One road goes to another legionary fortress at Deva, 139 Roman miles[1] to the north. We call it Chester now. Another goes to the Roman town of Venta Silurum (or Caerwent), nine Roman miles away near what we call the Bristol Channel. Another road leads westwards through what we call South Wales.

Outside the fortress are the huts of families who earn their living by keeping small shops where the soldiers can spend their pay. Each legionary receives about 300 *denarii* a year, but out of this he has to pay nearly fifty denarii for his bedding, clothes, armour and other equipment, and food. The clerks at headquarters tell him he should put some of his pay in the legionary savings

---

[1] A Roman mile was about 1,620 English yards; was it longer or shorter than our English mile?

bank, and Gaius and Julius try to save up at least five denarii each for the legion's annual dinner. Roman soldiers' uniforms are not provided with pockets, so when they go shopping they carry their money in a purse hung on one arm like the one in the picture. Some of it will be spent in the wine-shops, where they can sit down and talk while they drink, and sometimes they sing songs or listen to the old soldiers telling stories of the countries they saw and the battles they fought in when they were young men. Just now they are all talking about the Emperor's messenger. The shopkeepers are very pleased about this visit because people will flock in from all over the country-side to see the big military parade and the performances in the amphitheatre, and that means they will spend money in the shops.

The amphitheatre is outside the south-west gate and it is really a large oval open space, the *arena*, surrounded by low walls and a bank of earth on which are placed rows of wooden benches, one behind the other. If you have ever been to a circus with its *tiers of seats* round the circular arena, you will have some idea what the inside of the amphitheatre looks like. But there is no tent and the audience sits in the open air. Outside, a high stone wall props up the earth bank and prevents it from falling down under the weight of the seats. Entrances through the archways lead to the arena, or to flights of steps up to the seats.

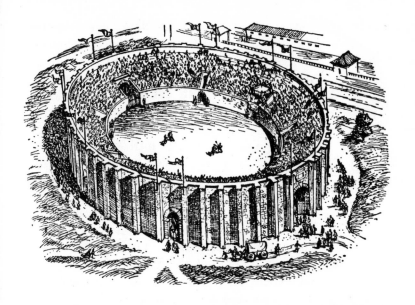

Here is the amphitheatre packed with people. Some seats are always reserved for the officers and any important visitors, but there is room for over 6,000 people, so all the legion and some of the countryfolk can crowd inside.

When the great day comes and the messenger from the Emperor arrives, the amphitheatre is crowded. The legionaries march in wearing their plumes in their helmets. They are led by standard-bearers carrying the standards, decorated today with garlands of flowers. Every soldier has polished his weapons and his armour until they sparkle and shine in the sunshine. Vibius Proculus has to frown sternly at his men because he is so proud of their appearance that he finds it difficult not to smile. They all belong to the Second Cohort, which is known to be one of the best in the legion, and Vibius's hardworked century looks the smartest in the cohort.

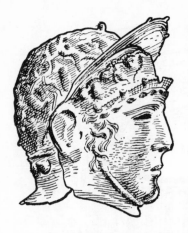

Now the Legate comes riding into the arena with the messenger and the other officers. They all wear armour with cloaks of gay colours, and their heads are covered with iron or bronze helmets gilded until they look like gold. You can see one in the picture. Even their faces are completely covered with shining metal masks, and when the country people see these they gasp with astonishment. The Legate inspects the troops and tells them that the Emperor's messenger is pleased with their drill and their smart appearance. He has already inspected the fortress and found it in good order, and he wishes to congratulate the builders, especially the mason Gaius of the century of Vibius Proculus. He will take back a good report of the Second Legion and probably the Emperor will find other work for them which will bring fresh glory to their standards. Meanwhile there will be wine so that every man can drink the Emperor's health that evening, and several days' holiday so they can all enjoy the entertainments in the amphitheatre.

These entertainments include sports. They may begin with competitions to see who can throw a spear or javelin the farthest, run the fastest, or wrestle the best. Conjurors and jugglers later appear and show off their tricks; other performers dance and sing and play musical instruments. But the items everyone is looking forward to most are the gladiatorial combats and the wild-beast show.

The *gladiators* fight each other with rather peculiar weapons. Sometimes one wears a big crested helmet and armour and fights with sword and shield against another man who has no armour, but is provided with a dagger and a *trident*, and a net in which he tries to entangle his opponent. A master of ceremonies carrying his staff of office sends on the gladiators, and the soldiers have bets with each other as to who will win the fight. Julius loses seven denarii and is very cross about it; his favourite gladiator fought much better at the last games and must be out of practice. When wild-beast shows come to Caerleon the animals do tricks, or else they fight each other or the gladiators fight them as well. Here is a picture of them doing it:

Small rooms near the entrances to the amphitheatre are used as cages for them before they go into the arena, and the arena walls are covered with a smooth cement so that the bears and lions cannot climb out and attack the audience. Many of the children have never seen bears and lions before and they talk about them for days. Everyone is sorry when the games are over and they all have to go back to work again.

WITH THE ARMY ON HADRIAN'S WALL

Meanwhile in the fortress the officers have been discussing the secret orders which the Emperor's messenger brought with him. When the Second Legion first came to Caerleon the tribes in the Welsh mountains were still battling against the Roman armies. Now that the big stone fortress is finished, this fighting is over and the legionaries in it need no longer be prepared to fight battles at short notice. The people living nearby, however, still need protection at times from the thieves who come down from the hills and try to steal their cattle.

Far away in the North of England the army are fighting large bands of tribesmen who come down from Scotland to the richer country further south, *looting* and burning and frightening the people. They are very difficult to catch, as a large number of soldiers would be needed to keep guard right across the country from Newcastle-upon-Tyne to Carlisle, far more than can be spared. The

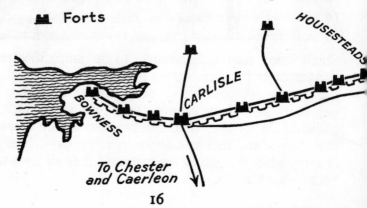

Forts

CARLISLE

HOUSESTEADS

BOWNESS

To Chester
and Caerleon

Emperor Hadrian himself has heard about this problem and in A.D. 122 came to Britain to see what can be done about it. He decided to build a great wall to keep out the raiders.

Look at the plan of the Wall below and find Wallsend at the mouth of the River Tyne. This is where Hadrian's Wall ended on the east coast; it ended on the west coast at Bowness on Solway, seventy-three miles away. Imagine building a big stone wall like this, seven to ten feet wide and twenty feet high with a rampart walk on the top, right across the country, up steep hills, across wild moors and over rivers. Tons of stones have to be collected, lime mortar mixed, and trenches dug for the foundations, before the building can even be begun.

Now the commander-in-chief at Caerleon has received orders for several cohorts of the Second Legion to go to the North of England and help with this work. The centurions are asked which of the men have done most building in stone. Vibius Proculus remembers how well Gaius worked on the barrack buildings and mentions his

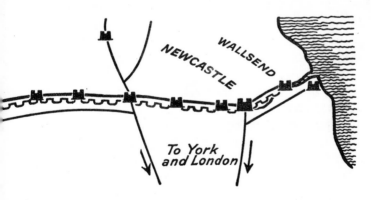

name. So Gaius finds himself promoted to be a centurion, and is told he will be in charge of one of the parties that will march north. At first he is worried at the thought that so much will depend on him, and he is sad at the idea of leaving Caerleon and Julius. Julius's time as a legionary is nearly up and soon he will retire. He hopes to settle down somewhere not too far from Caerleon, so that he can go back there and see those of his friends who still have some time to serve. Now he tells Gaius he is lucky to be setting out on such an adventure which will give him the chance of further promotion. There is nothing for him to worry about, the men of the Second Legion are far too well trained and alert to let anything interfere with their duty. Vibius Proculus, too, is very pleased about Gaius's promotion, and he gives him much good advice about leading a century on a long march, and organizing the work when he reaches Hadrian's Wall. Gaius thinks some of his ideas a bit old-fashioned, but he also feels it is very kind of him to try to help him.

Before he goes, Julius and his other friends give him a farewell party. They order oysters and some special wine called Falernian for the dinner, as well as pork and chicken. Before they start, they offer some of the wine and food to the goddess Fortuna so that Gaius may have good luck on the way. Then they eat and drink, and tell stories and sing songs, until Gaius goes back to barracks for the last time, very sleepy.

The following morning he is up early inspecting his men, and he is so strict with them that they say he is as bad as Vibius Proculus. Besides his weapons, every legionary has to carry all sorts of things on the march. One is a string bag for collecting any food he can find, or fodder for the animals. Then he has a sack full of rations and spare clothes, and a toolbag containing a saw, a *sickle*, a rope, a chain and stakes for the *palisade*, as well as the metal cooking pot and the saucepan for heating wine:

Imagine the noise all these things must have made as the soldiers marched along. The tents and the other heavy baggage are carried by two-wheeled carts drawn by horses or mules. Now the trumpets sound the advance, and Gaius and his century set out.

From Caerleon to the northern *frontier* where Hadrian's Wall is being built is a long way. Luckily there are good roads with paved or gravel surfaces already made, so the carts only get stuck in the mud occasionally. As soon as the legions first arrived in Britain in A.D. 43 they began to make these roads, and now the country south of the Wall is covered with a network of them, so that the army can get quickly from one place to another in case of trouble. Britain had no roads before the Romans came, only tracks trodden down where people often walked. The Roman roads were built of gravel, *flints*, or stones pressed well down on foundations of *rubble*, and sometimes they had ditches on either side. (You will find a diagram on page 78.) They were carefully planned by the trained legionary *surveyors*, who chose the best and shortest routes. Long after most people in Britain had forgotten the Romans, they went on using these roads, and it was only with the coming of the *turnpikes* in the eighteenth century that we learned how to build good roads again.

On their way north along the roads, Gaius and his comrades pass several camps and forts built by detachments of the Second Legion. Then they reach the town of Wroxeter near Shrewsbury, and there they are allowed several days' rest in which to lay in fresh supplies of food and enjoy visiting the baths and the shops. A few days later they reach the fortress at Chester, the home of the Twentieth Legion. They stay here for a time, and while the officers meet to make plans and discuss the latest news from the Wall, the men of the two legions compete with each other at spear-throwing, wrestling and other sports.

On such a long journey the legionaries cannot reach a camp or a fort every night. As they leave Chester and march north the danger from raiders increases and they have to take more and more precautions against surprise attacks. Setting up camp for the night is one of the things they have often practised and each century has its own tasks. They always compete to see who can get done the best and quickest.

Here is a picture of legionaries hard at work :

The walls of the camp are built of earth covered with *turf*. So some men start cutting the turves until they have a pile like the one you can see inside the walls. These walls are getting on well, but the soldiers are still carefully lifting the turves and putting them into position. One man is putting up wooden posts for a gateway. Others are busy digging a ditch outside the camp which will protect it against surprise attacks by raiders during the night. They place the earth in baskets which other men take away and empty. This is not a very popular job and two of the men in the ditch stop to grumble about it as soon as they realize they are hidden from sight by the wall. In another part of the camp, the baggage carts are being unloaded.

Now the men building the camp have got on so well they have only to put up the tents. These are made of

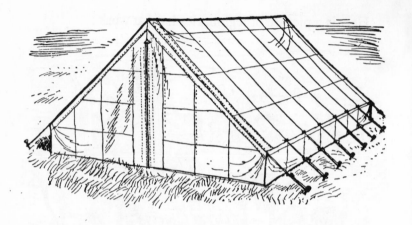

pieces of leather stitched together, and stretched over a framework of poles. The Latin name for the soldier's tent is 'papilio', meaning 'butterfly', because its sloping sides spread out from the centre of the roof like a butterfly's wings. We get our word pavilion from this. When it is folded and packed up it forms a roll like a caterpillar's *cocoon*. The officers have larger tents put up over folding frames rather like our garden tents. Meanwhile the cooks are busily at work cooking the supper in bronze saucepans and camp-kettles hung over the camp-fires and some of the men have gone to fetch water from a nearby spring.

At last the great day dawns and they reach their journey's end. A week ago some of the officers of the Second Legion went forward on horseback to prepare for their arrival, and now they come to meet them and guide them to a place where they can camp. This is in hilly country, in what we now call Northumberland, some miles west of Newcastle-upon-Tyne. After the busy fortress at Caerleon and Chester it seems very quiet and lonely. Gaius looks down from the high ground towards Scotland

and wonders how many fierce bands of raiders are even now on their way to attack them. A cold wind is blowing, and he shivers and wishes himself back with Julius singing songs by the cookhouse fire. Then he hears laughter and sees some soldiers marching back from their day's work and singing a song they are making up about their centurion. They seem happy enough and they make Gaius feel more cheerful.

The next day an officer comes to tell them about the latest plans for building the Wall. These have been drawn up by the engineers and approved by the Emperor Hadrian, and by Aulus Platorius Nepos, the governor of Britain. The great Wall must be guarded by a number of small *garrisons*, and these must have somewhere to live. So some very small forts called milecastles have to be built. They are called milecastles because they are a Roman mile apart.

Here is the plan of one of them. It is more or less square

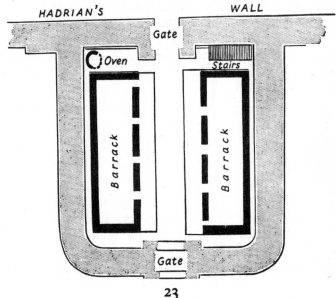

in shape with thick stone walls on three sides. These join on to Hadrian's Wall, which itself acts as the fourth wall. Inside are two small barrack buildings with room for up to fifty men. A road connects the two gates, one of which is an opening made right through Hadrian's Wall so that the soldiers can charge out quickly if necessary, and scatter any bands of enemies they may see approaching. The oven for the cooks is placed in one corner, and in the other a flight of steps leads up on to the rampart walk along the Wall. Here is a picture of what the milecastle probably looked like when the Second Legion had just finished building it :

Today we can still see the lower parts of the walls and part of the archways for the gates. The Romans built eighty milecastles along Hadrian's Wall, and we know that the Second Legion helped to build at least two of them (Nos. 37 and 38) because we have found pieces of the inscriptions they carved and put up when they had finished their work.

Two *turrets* about 540 yards apart were placed between each pair of milecastles. These are small watch-towers with ladders leading up to the rampart walk, where a few soldiers can camp in turn and keep watch. Here is a picture of what one probably looked like, imagined without one wall:

The men in the milecastles and turrets keep in touch with each other with smoke signals by day, or with fire signals at night. Apart from watching for armed raiders, they also act as frontier guards and customs officers. They must see that no loads of arms are smuggled through the frontier to help any gangs of thieves still at large further south, and they also keep an eye on the traders who go by travelling north, selling their goods to the tribes living far away beyond the Wall.

To help the watch, a wide flat-bottomed ditch between banks of earth is eventually dug a little way to the south of the Wall. This is called the *vallum* and it acts as the boundary of the military zone. Travellers going north are stopped at the vallum crossings, and then shepherded through the military area and out of one of the gates in the Wall. Travellers coming from the north are seen approaching by the guards, and if they are regarded as friendly and law-abiding, they in their turn are taken across the vallum. Here is a diagram showing the arrangement of the military zone and Hadrian's Wall:

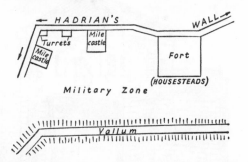

The men work hard and when they have any time off they begin to explore the countryside. Soon after their arrival Gaius asks "Who are the local gods?" as his century wish to make thank offerings for their safe journey. Silvanus is the Roman god who looks after the countryside and the wild animals far away from the towns, and here the local people call him Cocidius. So a small stone altar is made and put up in honour of Cocidius Silvanus by the grateful men of the Second Legion and offerings of wine are poured out before it.

While the legionaries are hard at work building the Wall and the milecastles and turrets, they are protected from the attacks of the raiders from across the frontier by a cohort of soldiers of a different type. They are called the *auxiliaries*: unlike the legionaries, they are not Roman

26

citizens. The legionaries do not all come from Italy, but they do come from the towns and villages of the more civilized parts of the Roman Empire and many of them are well-educated men. The auxiliaries are men conscripted from newly conquered tribes. They are sent away from their own countries to fight: can you think why the Romans do this? British auxiliaries went to fight along the German frontiers, and men from Germany, France, Spain, and the Near East all helped to defend the line of Hadrian's Wall.

Like the legions, auxiliaries are organized into centuries and cohorts, and other military formations. They are not trained craftsmen, so they do not do much building or road-making; instead they do more fighting, defending the legionaries who are busy constructing Hadrian's Wall and the labourers from other parts of Britain who have been sent to help them. Instead of the heavy armour and weapons of the legionaries, the auxiliaries use the weapons they are accustomed to in their own countries; they may have bows and arrows, clubs, or even slings. Often they wear short tunics and close-fitting trousers made of leather and they are protected by helmets and oval shields. Many of them are armed with a long, pointed sword, like the one this horseman is carrying.

His name is Rufus Sita and he is a Thracian. You can find out from the map on page 79 what a long way Thrace is from Britain. As well as his sword and shield, he carries a spear, and his conquered enemy lies on the ground with a broken sword in his hand.

After twenty-five years' service in the army, auxiliaries are discharged and become Roman citizens as a reward for their services. Then they are free either to go home again or to settle in the country where they have been fighting.

Some of the auxiliaries watched the offerings being made before the altar of Silvanus Cocidius and they may have told the legionaries about the nymph Coventina. She lives by the spring at Carrawburgh a few miles away and she brings good luck to all who go and worship her. As soon as Gaius has a chance he goes there to make offerings for himself and his century. The water from the spring runs into a square stone tank, and here is a picture of the carving of the nymph Coventina which stands beside it:

It shows her three times because she is so important—three times as powerful as the other local gods. She is always shown as pouring her precious water out of a bucket with one hand and holding up a cup of it with the other, and she sits on a leaf which floats on the water.

Except for the sound of the water it is very quiet by Coventina's spring and it is easy for Gaius to imagine as he recites his prayers that the goddess is somewhere round about listening to him. Slowly he drops some coins into the water, and then, because Coventina is shown as a young girl and probably like pretty things, he throws in some bronze brooches, bought from a pedlar he met on his way. Somehow he feels the goddess is pleased with his offerings and he goes away feeling happy.

When some of the milecastles and turrets are finished it is decided to build some larger forts, where the rest of the army can live in greater comfort and carry on their normal military training, while still being ready to go to their comrades' aid if necessary. One of these forts is built to the east of milecastles 37 and 38. It is marked on our diagram of the Wall as Housesteads, and probably the Second Legion helped to build it.

For the big stones which they needed they may have gone to Barcombe, a few miles south of Housesteads. We know the quarry here was used by the Romans because they have cut some of their names on the rocks. In one place we can still see the Latin words [P]ETRA FLAVI CARANTINI—"The stone of Flavius Carantinus".

Sometimes this rock was very difficult to cut, and on one expedition the men had a great deal of trouble trying to loosen some very hard stone. The centurion went to see what was wrong, and because he wanted his hands free he put down his arm-purse with three gold and sixty silver coins in it. He must have gone back to camp and forgotten where he put it, for it was found in the quarry by men cutting stone in 1837. Centurions were paid 5,000 denarii[1] a year, much more than the legionaries, but even so the poor man must have been very upset when he found he had lost it.

This is what the fort at Housesteads probably looked like when it was finished:

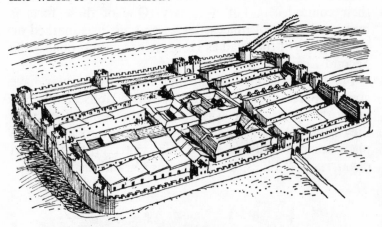

You can see Hadrian's Wall forming the north wall of the fort, and then going on its way to the east and west. The north gateway, cut through the Wall, can also be seen with a tower on either side. The lower parts of its walls and the outlines of the buildings can still be seen

[1] There were 25 denarii or silver coins to a gold coin.

today. Towers guard the gateways on the other three sides, and also the angles of the walls. The via principalis runs between the north and south gates, and passes the headquarters building, which is entered through an archway facing the road to the east gate. Through the archway you go into an open courtyard surrounded on four sides by a verandah. The usual rooms for the officers and the clerks lead off on three sides. A great hall runs the full width of the building on the fourth side. You can go into the hall either through another archway from the courtyard, or through small doorways leading off the side-streets. Here the commanding officer hears complaints and requests for leave, and issues punishments to defaulters. The centurions also meet here, and the non-commissioned officers have a meeting-place in one of the rooms leading off the courtyard. Beyond the hall are more offices and the *shrines* for the standards.

The two long low buildings next to headquarters on the side nearest to the north gate are the *granaries* where the corn supply for a year can be stored. The entrances are at the west end, where there is an open space in which carts can be unloaded without getting in the way of the troops or the traffic along the via principalis. On the other side of the headquarters is the house where the commanding officer lives with his family. This also has rooms built round the four sides of an open courtyard, and there is a door on the north side which opens opposite one of the side doors into the great hall. So the commandant is able to go from one to the other without having to come out into the main street. Another building built round a courtyard is the hospital, which lies behind the headquarters on our left. The other buildings are barracks and workshops.

Outside the fort the hillside is soon covered with little huts and shops. Some of them belong to the soldiers' families, others belong to people who feel safer living near the fort. They have cornfields and vegetable gardens, and can sell what they grow to the regimental canteen. Some of the shops sell wine to the soldiers or jewellery to their

wives. Shrines erected in honour of various gods are also built outside the fort. Mars, the god of war, was naturally worshipped by soldiers, and an altar like this one, showing him fully armed and wearing a helmet, probably stands in one of them.

Outside the fort you would notice at once the parade ground. This is about a hundred yards square, with a small turf-covered platform placed in the centre of one side. Here the legionaries practise their drill and weapon-training. Like the amphi-theatre at Caerleon, the parade ground is also used for sports, and as a place of assembly on such

solemn occasions as religious festivals. There are quite a number of these, but the most important one takes place at the New Year. Then the men parade in full-dress uniform with the standards decorated with garlands. They stand in front of altars dedicated to Jupiter the Best and Greatest (in Latin, Jupiter Optimus Maximus), the chief of the Roman gods, and they repeat their oath of allegiance. They ask Jupiter to protect the Emperor and his soldiers and give them victory, and they solemnly

swear to be loyal and faithful to their
Emperor and to work hard and fight
bravely for him and for the Roman
Empire. Every year fresh altars are
erected to the god with his name and
titles carved on them—IUPITER OPTIMUS
MAXIMUS—or I.O.M. for short as you
can see on this altar:

In his honour wine is poured out of special bronze
jugs into bronze dishes with long handles like these.

The old altars which were put up the previous year are
now reverently taken down and buried in a secret place
where no enemy can find them and make fun of them.
Then the men disperse, and enjoy the rest of the day as
a holiday.

LIVING IN TOWNS

Meanwhile life for Julius, whom we left behind at Caerleon, has been quite exciting. At first he missed Gaius very much, and the fortress, with so many legionaries away, seemed very dull and quiet. Then the time came for him to leave the army and he went to live in Caerwent or Venta Silurum, the market town of the tribe of the Silures, nine Roman miles away.

Julius spent much of his time with the legion making and repairing armour in the workshops, so now he buys a shop and sells small bronze articles which he makes himself. They include thin sheets of bronze decorated in various ways which are used as ornaments for wooden work-boxes and jewel-cases, small bronze nails, and brooches, pins, bracelets, and other jewellery. The brooches are great fun to make, for there are so many different kinds. The simplest ones are rather like our safety-pins, but there are also prettier shapes, some of them made in the form of birds or fish or animals or baskets of flowers, and enamelled in red and blue and green.

The pins sometimes end in tiny human heads or hands. The larger ones are used as hairpins. Sometimes girls use bone hairpins instead, but Julius says these break very easily while his bronze ones will last for ever. Luckily for him people are always losing their pins and brooches and then they have to buy new ones. Here are eight different pins that Julius might have made.

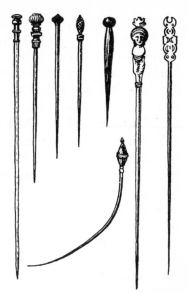

Julius lives in a little house not far from the *Forum*. Here is its plan:

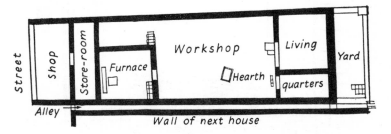

It is a long narrow building with one end opening on to the main street. This is the shop. A wooden counter stands at the entrance, otherwise it is just a room leading off the pavement.

Julius has folding wooden shutters which he puts up at night to keep out thieves. Behind the shops is a storeroom and then a big workshop with a furnace for heating the bronze and enamel. This is where he makes his brooches and other things. Two rooms lead off the workshop, and here he lives with the boy Victor who helps him serve in the shop and keep the furnace burning.

Stoking the furnace and hammering out the bronze is hot and dirty work so at the end of the day Julius and Victor shut up the shop and go along to the big bath-building a few yards down the street. You probably noticed that his own house has no bathroom; this is because everyone goes to the public baths nearly every day. We should call them Turkish baths. They are heated from a big furnace placed outside the hottest room which sends currents of hot air under the bathroom floors. The picture shows how these floors are raised and supported on columns of large flat tiles.

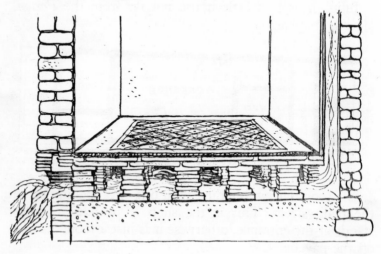

When the furnace is burning well they get so hot that the bathers have to wear sandals with thick soles, or their feet will get scorched. The hot air also finds its way up *flues* of hollow tiles built into the walls and warms these as well.

After Julius has given the bath attendant a coin called an *as* to pay for himself and Victor, they enter a big room where they undress and another attendant takes charge of their clothes. Then they go into a gently heated room where they meet several friends and sit and talk until they feel thoroughly warm and comfortable. From there they move into the hot room where the heat soon makes them begin to perspire. To encourage this perspiration Julius throws hot water over himself while Victor plunges into the small square bath full of hot water at one end of the room. Then Julius lies down on a marble slab and Victor scrapes the dirt off his skin with this curious bronze implement called a *strigil*. The Romans had no toilet soap, so Victor rubs Julius with some scented oils they brought with them in a bronze flask.

When they can bear the heat no longer, they come out first into the warm room to cool down and then go into an unheated room where they can have a good splash in a cold-water bath. After a brisk rub down they go back to the dressing-room feeling fresh and rested, and the attendant gives them their clean clothes. In summertime they wear sleeveless white tunics usually made of woollen cloth or linen, reaching below their knees and with a belt tied round the waist. Julius has a fine striped cloak which he fastens over his shoulder with one of his own brooches. The cloak has a hood he can pull over his head when the weather is cooler, and in wintertime he sometimes wears leather trousers.

Now Victor runs off to play with his friends while Julius takes a walk round the town. As he comes out of the baths he finds it is raining, so he crosses the road to the opposite pavement which is sheltered by a low sloping roof supported by pillars. A short way further on he turns right through a big archway into the big market-square called the Forum, which probably looked like the picture below. It also has pavements covered with a low sloping roof in front of the buildings. So here Julius can stroll about under cover. The low roof makes the buildings

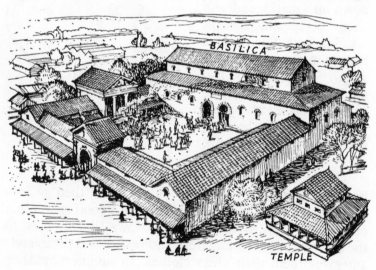

rather dark, but the small shops on two sides of the Forum have windows high up in their back walls to give them a better light. One shop is full of the shining red Samian pottery which has come all the way from France. Here are some Samian cups and bowls:

They are rather expensive to buy and the housewives have to save up their denarii until they can afford to add another plate or bowl to the best dinner service. They look after it very carefully, and if anyone is so careless as to break a Samian bowl, it is put together again and mended with lead rivets—unless it is too badly broken.

Another shop sells beautiful glass jugs and bowls in blue, green and amber and other pretty colours. These were also made in France and Western Germany, and some of the very delicate bowls may have travelled all the way from the Near East. You may think that some of these bottles have strange shapes:

Near the entrance to the Forum a pedlar is telling passers-by about the good strong mixing bowls he has for sale, piled up all around him. These thick earthenware bowls are called *mortaria* and are made in the potteries some miles away. The pedlar carries them from town to town packed in saddle-bags on the back of his donkey. Here is one of them:

In a sheltered corner Julius sees the public letter-writer at work. Most of the people in Caerwent still speak the Celtic tongue they spoke before the Roman armies came, but many of them also know a little Latin and the letter-writer is busy with letters and accounts in that language. Julius learnt to read and write in Latin when he joined the legion, so he does not have to pay anybody to write messages for him. The letter-writer uses a sharp-pointed object called a *stylus* and thin pieces of wood with one side covered with wax. He scratches the words on the

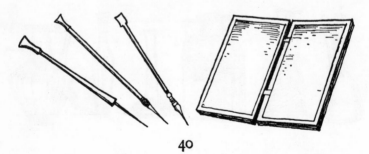

wax surfaces and when he makes a mistake he can rub it out with the other end of the stylus, which is blunt. When he has finished, the *tablets* are tied together so that the wax surfaces are inside. The man who is sending the letter puts wax on the knot in the cord and seals it with his signet ring. Sometimes he protects this seal with a little bronze box with an enamelled top like the one fastening this letter:

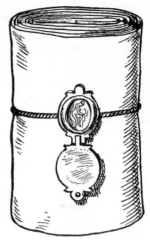

Julius makes many of these seal-boxes and he sees one of them being attached to a letter a shopkeeper is sending to a friend in another town, asking him to come and visit him in Caerwent.

It is raining heavily now and the water drips off the sloping roofs and gurgles merrily away along the gutters. Julius pulls his cloak more closely round him and goes in to see his friend the shoemaker. He is sitting at his bench surrounded by *lasts*. Here are some of the sandals and shoes and boots which he makes:

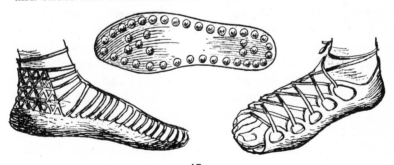

The boots have strong soles made of several thicknesses of leather studded with hobnails. The shoemaker is always busy, because people cannot help wearing out their shoes. "Something for your dainty little toes?" he suggests, looking at Julius's big soldier's feet. Julius laughs, and thinks he might make him some slippers like the purple pair with gilt edges which are waiting for a rich lady to send her maid to collect them. "This is what I enjoy making most," says the shoemaker, "scarlet slippers for a little girl's birthday. I shall just get them finished before I start on some new boots for the magistrate. He ordered them this morning before he went into the *Basilica* and he is still in court there. Poor man, he must be tired!"

As the shoemaker is so busy, Julius thinks he will go and see what is happening in the Basilica. On his way there he moves into the middle of the market-place to avoid the smell from the fishmonger's shop at the foot of the steps. Not only does he sell oysters and mussels, but he also fries fish for people to take away. Many of the citizens wish he would move his shop from the Forum to one of the quieter streets outside.

The Basilica is the most important building in the town. It is 162 feet long and occupies one complete side of the Forum. Inside, the high roof is supported by two rows of columns with carved *capitals*, so that the space is divided into a *nave* and two *aisles*, rather like our churches. The floor is of reddish concrete, and the walls are plastered and painted in gay colours, chiefly red and yellow.

Julius goes in through a door into the south aisle and walks up the central hall or nave. He has often been here for public meetings, but today the few people in the Basilica are standing round the raised platform or *Tribunal*

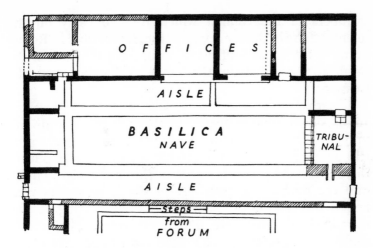

at one end where the *Magistrate* is sitting. You can find where he is sitting from this plan.

The Magistrate is trying to settle a case about the property left by a man who died a short time ago. He married twice, and now his eldest son is quarrelling with his step-mother about his father's money. He has disliked her for years and is enjoying telling everybody what he thinks of her, and she is also being very nasty to him whenever she can get a word in edgeways. At last the magistrate interrupts them and says it is growing too late for him to make up his mind tonight. He will listen to them again tomorrow, and then give his judgement.

The townsfolk elect the magistrates and at election times there is great excitement, with everyone trying to persuade people to vote for their favourite. Some of the shopkeepers paint posters on their walls saying "Vote for Flavius, he will reduce the taxes" or perhaps "Support Sempronius, he will build us new baths". When magistrates retire they become '*decurions* of the *ordo*', that is, members of the council which tries to carry on the town's affairs in the same way as the Senate does in Rome. Some of the council offices lead out from the back of the Basilica; they include the council chamber and the treasury.

The magistrate and his attendants leave the Basilica. Julius slowly follows them out through the Forum and into the street. The rain has stopped, so he decides he will go along to the temple to see the new statue put up there a few days ago. He goes in through a big archway into the temple courtyard. After the busy streets with horses and carts rattling along and all the talking people, it is very peaceful here under the trees. The temple shown in the picture of the Forum and Basilica on page 38 is a small square building built out into a semicircle or *apse* at one end and surrounded by a *colonnade* consisting of a low sloping roof supported by columns standing on a low wall. Today we can only see the foundations of the walls outlined in the turf like two squares, one inside the other:

But when Julius saw the little temple, it was complete with its columns and red tiled roof. Inside it is rather dark and mysterious. The walls are painted in stripes of red, white and yellow, and the floor is covered with small squares of tiles called *tesserae*, which are fixed in a layer of cement. A shaft of light falls on the stone statue of the god Mars, also brightly painted. It stands on a *pedestal* in the apse. Julius, as an old soldier, has worshipped Mars as the god of war for many years, and now he stands looking at his statue remembering how he used to go with his friends to make thank-offerings at his altars in Caerleon whenever they had been out chasing raiders away into the hills. But Mars is a very powerful god and he is willing to look after the affairs of his worshippers in peace-time as well as in battle. Here his statue stands on a pedestal bearing an inscription saying that it was erected to Mars Lenus and the Divinity of the Emperor by some of the shopkeepers in Caerwent, to show how grateful they are for not having had to pay any taxes for several years.

Julius watched a procession of them bring the statue to the temple a few days ago, but this is the first time he has had a chance to look at it closely. He thinks the sculptor has done a good piece of work. Surely the god will be pleased and go on looking after the worshippers! We do not know whether we would agree with Julius, for only the feet of the statue still exist: they stand on the pedestal on which we can see the inscription.

A few days later Julius meets his friend Marcus Valerius. Marcus asks him to come to dinner that evening. Marcus is a decurion, and because he has just been to a

meeting of the ordo he is wearing his *toga*. This is a large piece of woollen material worn draped over the left shoulder so that one end touches the feet and the other is carried round the back, under the right arm, across the chest and the left shoulder, and then allowed to hang down the back almost to the feet. It is a very dignified garment and it has to be arranged very carefully, otherwise it might come unwound or the wearer might fall over it. Here is Marcus wearing his toga. Marcus and Julius are proud of the fact that they are Roman citizens, and therefore have the right to wear the toga, but Julius, as a busy man leading a very active life, really prefers to wear his cloak and keep his toga for special occasions.

He wears his toga that evening, however, as he walks to Marcus's big house just inside the west gate. A servant meets him at the entrance and takes him into the inner courtyard where Marcus's children are playing ball. They come running up to greet him and beg him to tell them a story. "Tell us about when you were a soldier and chased the raiders into the mountains for miles and miles and miles!" "Another time," says Julius, "your father is waiting for me now", and he follows the servant into the house as Marcus comes to look for him. He unwinds his toga with a sigh of relief. A servant brings a basin and a jug of scented water, takes his sandals, and washes his hands and feet, and another offers him a wreath of flowers. Instead of sitting at a dining-table, he and Marcus lie on couches, leaning on their left elbows and propped up by a pile of cushions. Do you think that Julius looks comfortable?

Julius is the only guest because Marcus has something he particularly wants to talk to him about, but first they will have dinner. The servant comes back and puts a tray of food on a small three-legged table between them. There are oysters and stuffed eggs and other titbits. These are followed by roast lamb and the first of the season's beans, boiled chicken and parsley sauce, and a ham. Then there is a sweet made of pastry and honey, and some fruit. They talk about the new baths Marcus has promised he will build for the town, about the progress of the great Wall in the north, and about how quickly the children are growing up. Then the servants clear the table, except for the jug of wine and the glass cups, and leave the two friends alone.

Marcus comes straight to business. He reminds Julius that a wealthy friend of theirs died recently, leaving all his possessions to his only daughter and asking Marcus to settle up his affairs. The daughter, Julia, is the wife of a farmer who lives in another part of Britain, near the big city of Verulamium. Marcus has sold his old friend's house and packed up the furniture and other household goods, and now he is trying to arrange for them to be sent to her. He can hire wagons to carry the packages and he has plenty of servants to drive the horses, but he must have someone he can trust to take charge of the party. He cannot get away himself. Would Julius go in his place? Of course, he would be well paid, and would enjoy the journey and the chance to see all the fine new buildings which are being built all over the country.

Julius does not hesitate. Victor can look after his shop while he is away and Marcus will keep an eye on Victor. Certainly he will go. Marcus gets a map and they discuss the journey. If you look at the map of Roman Britain on page 83 and find Venta Silurum (Caerwent) and Verulamium (near St. Albans in Hertfordshire), you will be able to see which way the party had to go. They will not be able to travel very quickly with the heavily laden carts. Sometimes they will reach a town for the night and then Julius will be able to stay at the inn, or he may be able to visit friends of Marcus who have big country-houses near the main roads. There are small inns also in some of the villages where travellers stop to change horses, but for the rest of the time they will have to camp out, and this is where Julius's training as a soldier will be so useful. There will be no need to build a rampart to protect the party, but he will have to tell the servants who is to cook, find water and firewood, and look after the horses.

When the time comes to leave, the wagons are stacked high with packages and the drivers climb up and gather up the reins. Marcus has lent Julius a light two-wheeled carriage in which he will be able to travel ahead more quickly to warn the innkeepers of his party's arrival, or else he can stay behind in the towns paying for his food and stores and then catch the wagons up again. Here are the horses, anxious to be off:

They rumble out of the gate of Caerwent and take the road to Glevum, or Gloucester, a town Julius is looking forward to visiting because the Second Legion was stationed there before it went to Caerleon in A.D. 75. This was some years before he joined the legion, but he used to hear the old soldiers talk about it when he was a young man. He sees the site of the old legionary fortress as he crosses the River Severn. It proved so damp that now only quays and a few wooden huts and offices are built there, and the town which has taken its place is built on higher ground.

Gloucester is a *colonia*, a city specially founded by the Roman government as a place where *veteran legionaries* can retire and show the native populations what town life is like. There were no towns in Britain before the Romans came, but by the second century the Britons are already taking a pride in them and enjoy their fine new baths and other public buildings. Every *citizen* in a colonia owns a piece of land outside the city walls where he can grow his own food, and they all have the right to vote for the four magistrates elected each year to look after the affairs of the town.

From Gloucester, Julius and his party travel south-east along the road to the Roman town at Corinium, or Cirencester. They pass several large country-houses belonging to Marcus's friends on the way. The ruins of one of these Roman villas can still be seen at Witcombe today. Each villa is surrounded by cornfields, orchards and flower gardens, and the travellers receive a warm welcome. Julius gives the owner of one house two new books which Marcus has sent him. His secretary has carefully copied them out in ink on long rolls of parchment which are then rolled up and sealed. Since printing is not known, all books have to be written out by hand like this. They are read until the reader almost knows them off by heart. Two new books at once is a very exciting present.

Cirencester is the market town of the tribe called the Dobuni and it is a very rich and busy place. Julius stays with another friend of Marcus in a big well-furnished house. Several rooms have *mosaic* floors made of hundreds of little cubes of stone and tiles called tesserae. They are of different colours and arranged in various designs. Probably one floor shows the god Orpheus playing his *lyre*, with his dog frisking beside him and a procession of birds and animals walking around them. Mosaics of this kind (but probably made in the third or fourth centuries) are on view in the Corinium Museum at Cirencester today, and there we can see a lion, a leopard, a tiger, and other animals all enjoying the music.

Several days later the party moves on again, travelling through more pretty country with farmers hard at work in the fields. After they leave the little Roman town at Alchester in modern Oxfordshire, however, the road goes through forests and they meet very few people. Only the milestones—which each have the Emperor's name and the number of miles to Verulamium carved on them—remind Julius that the end of the journey is now in sight, as the farm they are going to is only a few miles from that city.

At last they can see the buildings of Verulamium in the distance. They come out on the great Roman main road, which is now called Watling Street. It starts in Kent, passes through London, and goes right up through the Midlands to Wroxeter in Shropshire and other places farther north. It is a very busy road, with country-folk taking their fruit and vegetables to sell in the city, and travellers on horseback or in carts and wagons on their way to all sorts of places.

Verulamium is one of the oldest towns in Britain. Even in the first century A.D. it was so important that the Roman government probably made it a *municipium*, with the right to elect annually four magistrates (called *quattuor-viri*). These were much the same as the magistrates elected by the citizens of a colonia. The chief difference between a colonia and a municipium was the fact that a colonia was a town founded by the Roman government, while a municipium was a city founded by the people themselves which became so important that the government felt they must recognize it. So far as we know, Verulamium was the only municipium in Britain and the people who lived there must have been very proud of it.

As Julius walks through it he notices all the usual land-marks of a Roman town: the Forum, shops, several temples, and some very fine big houses. Instead of the stone walls he is used to seeing at Caerleon and Caerwent, he finds that these buildings have walls of flint and mortar with layers of bright red tile. This is because there is no good building-stone near Verulamium. When limestone was used for one of the temples it had to come from forty or fifty miles away, and must have been very expensive. Many of the walls are plastered outside and painted red or white, and most of the houses have painted wall decorations in the chief rooms indoors. The house where Julius stays has a red and green colour scheme and a lovely mosaic floor in the dining-room showing this *scallop-shell* design worked in red, yellow, black, blue and white:

In another house he sees a new floor just finished; this has a picture of the head of the sea-god, Oceanus, in the middle. The god has a beard and wild seaweed-like hair with red lobster claws growing out of it. The pavement has a border with flowers and tall vases with handles in alternate squares. Here is Oceanus:

Julius enjoys looking at the shops. They are full of lovely things brought from all over the Roman Empire. He even sees some silk which has come all the way from China, and

elephant *tusks* from Africa. He studies very carefully the latest fashions in brooches and bracelets in the jewellers' and bronze-workers' shops, as he wants to take some new ideas home to Caerwent. He is amazed at the beautiful gold and silver necklaces, some of them studded with *sapphires*, *amethysts* and other precious stones. Compare this jewellery with Julius's brooches and pins on pages 34 and 35.

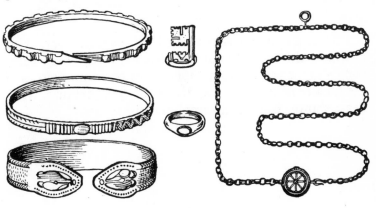

Instead of an amphitheatre the people of Verulamium have built themselves a real theatre. It has a wooden stage and a curtain which is raised and lowered by balancing it with heavy weights. Richly carved stone columns separate the stage from the arena and one of these can still be seen among the ruins of the theatre today. You can see it in the picture:

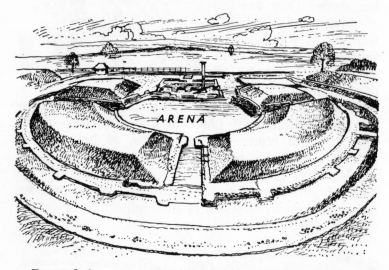

Part of the arena is covered by a wooden floor. This is where the orchestra sit. Occasionally travelling companies come across from France and perform plays, and the theatre is used at other times for cock-fighting, wild-beast shows, and all the amphitheatre sports.

STAYING AT A ROMAN VILLA

Early one morning Julius collects his party for the last time, and they set out from Verulamium for the villa of Flavius Tiburtinus, near the modern town of Welwyn. They do not reach it till late in the day, and when they first see the house its red roof and colour-washed walls are lit up by the rays of the setting sun. The watch-dogs rush out barking as they come along the lane through the barley fields, and Flavius Tiburtinus comes to welcome them. He thinks it is too late to begin unloading the wagons that night, as they must all be very tired. His servants will look after the horses and they must come in and have a meal.

The Romano-Britons usually go to bed soon after sunset and get up early in the morning so as to make the most of the daylight. At night, candles and small oil-lamps are their only means of lighting the houses, and people carry lanterns or flaming torches when they have to go out. Julius lies down to his supper in the dining-room near a table on which stand several of the little pottery lamps. They are just little bowls with one or more spouts and a fixed cover, called a *discus*, instead of a lid. The oil is poured in through a small hole in the discus and the wick is placed in the spout.

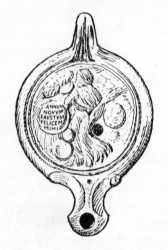
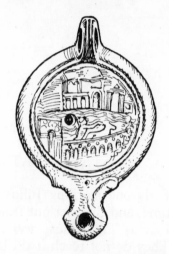

The discus is decorated in various ways, and here you can see two of them. The one on the right is decorated with a picture of a big city. In the foreground there is a bridge over a river and a man driving his donkey over the bridge. The lamp on the left has a figure of Victory shown as a woman carrying a shield, and with

coins, nuts, and cakes lying round her feet. On the shield is written in Latin ANNUM NOVUM FAUSTUM FELICEM MIHI, and this means "I wish myself a Happy New Year". Really it is a lamp which was bought some years ago to bring good luck at the New Year to all the household. The coins, nuts and cakes are New Year presents. Now he tells Julius to take it with him to his bedroom. He will find an iron lamp-holder for it fixed on to his bedroom wall.

56

The next morning Julia is up early. She wishes to make a good impression on Julius, so her maids bring her scented water to wash with, rub her with perfumed oils, and help her to dress.

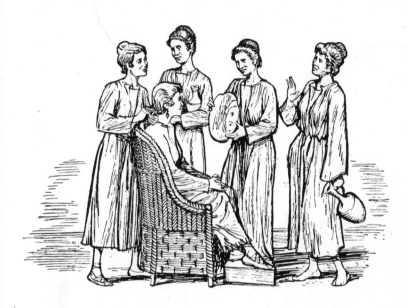

She wears a long-sleeved under-tunic and over it a blue *stola*, a sleeveless dress reaching to her feet with a *flounce* stitched round the hem. One of her maids ties the *girdle* round her waist and then she sits down in her basket-chair while another maid arranges her hair. At this time the fashionable ladies at court are wearing their hair divided into a number of small plaits, pinned up round their heads or piled up into a *coronet*. The hair in front may be waved or curled in a number of different ways, and if yours is not naturally thick enough to make a good show you just send your maid out to buy some more. Julia, a farmer's wife, cannot yet experiment with these elaborate hairstyles, although now that she is wealthy she promises herself she will find out if any hairdresser is doing them in Verulamium. For the present she must be content with having her maid coil her thick red hair into a bun, fasten it with black jet hairpins, and curl it in front with the curling-irons. This takes some time as the girl is not very clever, and every time she singes a curl or pulls the hair Julia scolds her. Everyone is thankful when the hairdressing is finished and another maid can pluck her eyebrows, manicure her hands and paint her face with red ochre and white chalk. Here is Julia's comb and her bronze tweezers and manicure set:

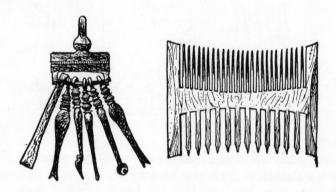

Then Julia unlocks her jewel-box with a key which is fastened on to a ring which she can wear on her finger, and puts on a gold chain and several brooches. She puts on some of her best bracelets too. She would buy her jewellery at Verulamium, and the picture on page 53 will remind you what it looked like. The maids fasten on her sandals, drape a light cloak round her, and give her a

handkerchief and a fan. One maid walks behind her carrying her parasol. Here it is, on the right, and the fan is on the left. At last the lady of the house is prepared to face the world.

By this time the wagons that Julius escorted here have almost been unloaded, and Julia is soon rejoicing in her new possessions. She forgets to be a grand lady, and puts aside the fan and the parasol as she helps her maid sort out her mother's Samian dinner service. It has arrived without a crack, and not one glass jug or bowl is chipped or broken. How careful Julius must have been in stopping the wagons going too fast over bumpy roads, and the drivers must be well rewarded for packing their loads so well. Here is her father's silver bowl—the sight of it nearly makes her cry as she remembers she will never see him use it again. The beautifully carved wooden couches with their mattresses, covers and cushions will go in the dining-room. Flavius can have the little cupboard for his *book-scrolls*. This small table with its three bandy legs decorated with lions' heads she will put in her own room. All the cushions, blankets and other coverings had better be well aired in the garden; then they can be packed away in the chests in the storeroom.

While Julia is putting everything in its new place, Julius tells her how difficult it was for Marcus to decide what to sell for her in Caerwent and what to send to her to use in her home. He knew that brushes and brooms and dusters for the maids would be useful, and so would be the bronze pans, jugs, and strainers for the kitchen. The cook does most of the cooking over small *charcoal* fires on clay hearths, standing the pans and pottery bowls and jars on iron *tripods* and *gridirons*. There is a new gridiron for him, some big hooks from which to hang meat, a frying-pan, a chopper, knives, of all sizes, and a *ladle*. Which of these can you find in the picture?

The money from the sale of the house is locked away by Flavius in his big wooden treasure chest. Its feet are cemented into the floor so that no-one can run away with it.

When the unloading is finished, Flavius takes Julius to see the farm. The land has belonged to his family for many years, but before the Roman invasion in A.D. 43 the farmhouse was only a small hut built of wood and *wattle and daub*. By the middle of the first century Flavius's great-grandfather thought he would like to try more Roman ways, so he built a house with foundations of

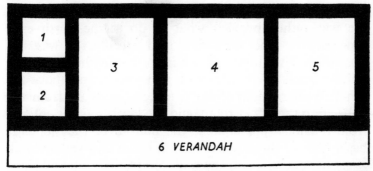

PLAN OF FIRST ROMAN HOUSE

layers of flint and lumps of chalk laid alternately in a trench. On these were built flint and mortar walls twenty-eight inches thick. The upper parts of the walls were probably of wood, and so were the thin partition walls which divided the rooms. These looked out on to a verandah with a sloping roof supported by wooden posts.

Flavius thought this house was much too small, and if you look carefully at the two plans on this page, you will see how he enlarged it.

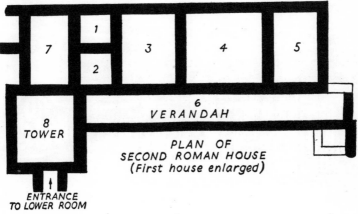

PLAN OF
SECOND ROMAN HOUSE
(First house enlarged)

ENTRANCE
TO LOWER ROOM

61

He decided to extend it by adding rooms at each end. He was rather puzzled what to do at the north end, however, for the ground sloped steeply. It was not possible to level it off or bank it up. Finally he decided to build a small tower there with two rooms, one above the other. A short flight of wooden steps leads up from the house into the upper room, and the lower room is entered from outside by a door at the bottom of the slope. It has a floor of tiny squares of red, green and yellow brick stuck in concrete, and the walls are painted red and black on a white background. The upper parts of the walls of the house are of wood, with wattle and daub packed in between the beams and plastered and painted pink on the outside. The wooden verandah has been replaced by one with small pillars and low flint walls and the roof is covered with gay red tiles. This picture shows what it probably looked like:

If Flavius and his wife had known she was going to inherit some money so soon, they would have waited and built a more elaborate house. But when he planned this one he was trying not to spend too much money on it, so he used materials for building which he and his men could find close at hand. Julia hopes that now they can have some baths added. Flavius is not very keen to have the baths as part of the house. He is afraid of fire. It is different in places like Caerwent where people can use stone for building. But much of this house is of wood, and Flavius knows that heat escaping from a leak in the tile channels or from under a raised floor might start the wooden beams smouldering. Julius suggests that he should build a separate little bath-house a short way from the villa.

Then Julia hopes they will be able to have some really exciting mosaic floors. There is an artist in Verulamium who designs them and last time she went to that city he showed her his books of patterns. A villa in the south where she once stayed with her father had some lovely designs. On one appeared this picture of the goddess Venus wearing a head-dress and a *chaplet* of flowers and with a peacock on either side of her. A border of winged *cupids* pretending to be gladiators formed part of the same pavement.

A mosaic in another room showed the eagle carrying off the boy Ganymede from Mount Ida in Greece, where he was watching his father's sheep, to Olympus because Jupiter wanted him for his cupbearer. Ganymede is wearing a red cap, cloak, and boots, and you can see he is still clutching his shepherd's crook. Another mosaic had pictures of the Seasons, shown as girls, with birds and flowers and ears of corn. Today only Winter remains, an older woman well wrapped up against the cold and carrying a bare branch, as you can see below.

This villa that Julia visited was at Bignor in Sussex; if you ever visit it for yourself, you will see all these mosaics and also one showing cupids as gladiators.

Flavius would rather save money for the children's education than spend it on mosaic floors. If they lived in a town his children would have started going to school when they were seven years old. At school they would learn to read and write and do simple arithmetic. Much of their time would have been spent learning by heart the alphabet, numbers, and the simple things they read and copied out, and reciting them aloud.

School started at daybreak, schoolmasters were usually very strict, and inattention, forgetfulness, unpunctuality and other faults were severely punished. Two hundred years later we find the fourth-century writer Ausonius reminding his little grandson in a letter that "the sour schoolmaster's voice does not always harass boys" and some days are holidays. If he learns readily he need never be afraid even if the school echoes with many a stroke of the cane. His father and mother went through all this when they were children and now they are the joy of his grandfather's old age.

Flavius's villa is too far away from Verulamium for Faustus, Tiberius, and Aelia to be able to attend school daily. Since he has not been able to afford the price of an educated slave to act as tutor, Julia has been teaching them to read and write. Now he thinks he might send Faustus, who is nearly twelve years old, to live with his uncle in Verulamium, where he would have a chance of a better education. At twelve he can go to a more advanced school where he will read much Latin literature and learn to write essays and verses about what he has read. We are not sure which books he will study, but like children learning Latin today they probably include Cicero's speeches and the poetry of Virgil, Ovid, and Horace. Perhaps Faustus will also learn Greek, and geometry and arithmetic in case he becomes an important merchant as Julia's father used to be. He is unlikely to go on to the school of the *rhetor* when he is older. There the students spend all their time learning the art of public speaking and discussion. Only the sons of very wealthy men who will never have to earn their own living or who hope to be lawyers and magistrates can afford this.

Tiberius is still too young to go to school, so Julia will go on teaching him with his elder sister Aelia. The little girl of ten years old is already beginning to help her mother run the house and arrange the work for the maids. She is learning to weave and spin, as most of the cloth used for clothes is woven at the villa and only the stuff for some of Julia's dresses is bought in Verulamium. Already Aelia can spin the wool shorn from her father's sheep and she knows which plants to use to dye the cloth when it is finished. The family talk Latin together, but only a few of the servants understand it, so Aelia and her mother often have to speak to them in the old British language.

66

The children romp together in the garden and in the woods near the villa. They have balls and hoops, several pet dogs, a tame bird, and a kitten. Aelia looks after several dolls and toy animals, and Tiberius's favourite toy is a little cart. Sometimes they play at *knuckle-bones* with the small bones found just above the hooves of cloven-footed animals. The knuckle-bones are thrown up into the air and the player tries to catch as many as possible on the back of her hand. If she misses any, she has to pick them up from the ground with the same hand without dropping any of the bones she has caught on the back of it. Dice were also thrown and used with counters and pieces, and several games rather like our draughts or back-gammon were played by grown-ups as well as children.

After Julius has been shown round the house he follows Flavius out into the yard. If the weather keeps fine the harvest will be ready for reaping next week and several men are hard at work getting ready for it. The carpenter is re-pairing several carts with tools very like those used by craftsmen today. He has hammers and chisels, *gouges* and a *plane*, but his iron saw-blade is not as good as the steel saw we can go out and buy. How does he use each of these tools?

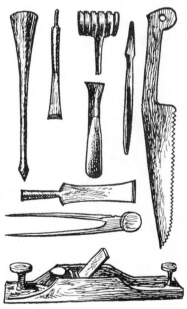

Nearby the smith is making some new *sickles*, holding the iron in his big smith's *pincers* as he heats it in the furnace, and then hammering it out on his anvil. Beside him lie a pile of *scythes* brought in by the haymakers. He has had no time to repair them and some of them have worn or broken blades which need riveting or patching. Some only need sharpening, and a few will have to have their blades completely replaced. The blades can be sharpened again with *hones* on the special little *anvils* which the haymakers carry about with them. Here are some of the tools made by the smith:

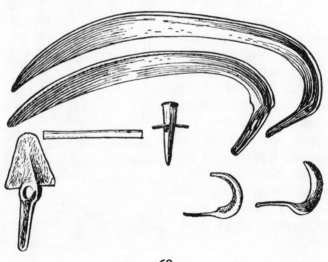

Julius is used to the big legionary workshops, and this little country *smithy* does not interest him very much. He begins to talk of his journey back to Caerwent. He is afraid that he and Marcus's servants will be eating Flavius out of house and farm. But Flavius begs him to stay a little longer. Few people come past his villa and he is very much enjoying his visit. Why don't they all stay and give him a hand with the harvest next week and join in the party afterwards? Julius accepts the invitation with pleasure. He wants to get home to Caerwent before the autumn days grow too short for long journeys, but he can certainly spare another week. Meanwhile, he will send a messenger to Verulamium to see if any of Marcus's friends there can find him a load for the wagons to carry back home.

Next morning he goes hunting in the woods near the villa. As he rides along he wonders if he will have a chance of throwing a spear at a wild boar, but he is unlucky. By the end of the day he has only bagged two deer. Four of the servants go out and bring them home for him slung from two poles. The children look forward to roast *venison* for dinner.

The first day of the harvest dawns warm and fine and everyone is up very early and is soon out to work in the fields. The corn is cut off just below the ear with small sickles and put in sacks and baskets. These are piled up in the wagons and brought back to the farm, where the corn is spread out to dry. The weather rarely keeps fine long enough for it to dry thoroughly, so many farms build special corn-drying ovens. These are built rather like the bath-house with raised floors under which passes hot air heated by a furnace. The floors have to be built in two layers with a space between so that they do not get too hot and cause the corn to catch fire. Unlike the army in the forts and fortresses, the farmers cannot afford well-aired granaries built of stone, so they store the grain in barns and deep clay-lined pits. Several new pits have to be dug every year as the old ones are apt to turn mouldy after being in use for several seasons. Then the household rubbish is buried in them instead.

At last the harvest is safely in and the household settle down to feasting and jollification. They go out in a procession singing hymns of thanksgiving to the gods of the fields and woods who have looked after them so well. Here are the little figures of the household gods:

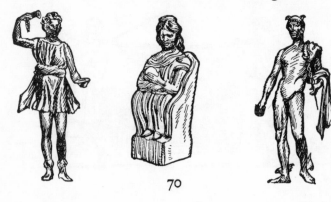

They live in a shrine in a cupboard in the house, and on special feast days they are taken out and wreathed with flowers. There is the Lar with his horn of plenty, and small *statuettes* of Mercury and a mother goddess. They are all offered food and wine before the feasting starts, and then everybody really gets down to the business of eating as much as possible. Afterwards they dance and sing and play games, and so it goes on for several days of happy holidaymaking.

They are just going rather wearily back to work when a messenger arrives with a letter for Julius. It tells him that several loads of cloth are to go to Caerwent: he is to pick them up in Verulamium. He calls for Marcus's servants, and they begin to get everything collected for an early start the next morning. As dawn breaks, the horses are harnessed to the wagons. Flavius and Julia thank him again for coming and the children run beside his carriage as he drives down the lane, crying "Vale, vale, vale"—

"Farewell, farewell, farewell".

HOW DO WE KNOW ABOUT THE PEOPLE WHO
LIVED IN ROMAN BRITAIN?

IT IS more difficult to find out about Roman Britain than about later times in English history because in the second century A.D. no-one in Britain had begun to write down what was happening. There are no history books or letters or diaries to help us at all. So we have to find out in other ways. Some of the people who spend their time searching round the country for clues are called *archaeologists*. They often carry spades with them. If you do not already know why, you will soon find out.

I. WHAT WE CAN FIND OUT IN OUR OWN COUNTRY

1. *From Inscriptions and Tombstones*

A large number of stones with Latin inscriptions put up in Roman times can still be seen. They are mostly in museums, but new ones go on turning up in places where the Romano-Britons lived. They are very important to us because they are the only written records we have dating from this period. Some of them tell us about work being done and who did it. It may have been the army—and we have already heard about some of the inscriptions put up by the Second Legion along Hadrian's Wall—or the town councils when they built baths and other important buildings.

It is very exciting to dig up bits of stone with letters on them and to try to fit them together like a jig-saw puzzle. Thus, at Wroxeter, near Shrewsbury, pieces of stone with traces of lettering were collected and fitted together. From this we know that the tribe called the Cornovii placed a large inscribed tablet in honour of the Emperor Hadrian over the main entrance to their Forum, telling everyone that this building was erected in A.D. 130. Sometimes we can see the names of gods and goddesses inscribed on their altars and we can often discover the names of people from their tombstones. These may also tell us the name of the person who put up the stone, the name of the dead person's father or his rank in the army.

For example, we learn from the inscription on a tombstone found at Caerleon that it was erected

> To the memory of Gaius Valerius Victor, son of Gaius of the Galerian tribe from Lugdunum, company standard-bearer in the Second Augustan Legion. He served for seventeen years and lived forty-five years. Set up under the direction of his heir Annius Perpetuus.

Lugdunum was the Latin name for Lyons in France, so Victor's father must have come from near there.

Some of the tombstones also show carved portraits of the dead person and from these we can discover what kind of clothes the people wore, how they did their hair, and the kind of tools they used. Our picture on page 68 is copied from a smith's tombstone found at York, and the Thracian auxiliary Rufus Sita on page 27 can be seen carved on a stone now in the Gloucester Museum. Sometimes the whole family appears on the tombstone or the dead person is shown alone enjoying a meal. At Chester a lady called Curatia Dionysia may be seen doing this, lying on a couch with a high back, her arm supported by a pile of cushions. Her position is like our picture on page 47. A small table stands in front of her and she holds a cup of wine in her right hand. Curatia was only forty years old when she died.

2. *How we find the places where people lived*

We have already looked at some of these—the fortress at Caerleon, the fort at Housesteads, the towns at Caerwent and Verulamium, and the villa at Lockleys near Welwyn where Flavius lived. How did anyone know they were there? One reason is because the Romano-Britons built so well that some of their walls are still standing. You can see the ruins of the great walls and gates at places like Colchester, Caerwent, Verulamium, Lincoln, York or London, and you can walk along Hadrian's Wall and see the sites of many other forts, turrets and milecastles besides the ones near Housesteads.

The map on pages 16–17 shows the whole length of Hadrian's Wall. The main forts are marked, and between these were the smaller milecastles. There were several forts to the north of the Wall, and one Emperor had a wall built even further north. But the Romans could not hold this second wall for long against the wild tribes.

We must remember the Roman legions landed here in A.D. 43 and Britain was part of the Roman Empire until some time in the first half of the fifth century. Building of various kinds was going on during the whole of that period. People who lived after the Romans found the Roman work very useful when they wanted materials for their own castles and houses, so we can often find Roman tombstones, inscriptions, squared building stones or tiles used in the walls of churches. Many Roman buildings fell down as the result of this stone-robbing, but no doubt the later builders were very pleased to be able to get stone so easily without the trouble of cutting it for themselves.

Sometimes the people took all the stones, so that nothing of the Roman building can now be seen above the surface of the ground. The Romans themselves also found stone too expensive when they had to bring it from a long distance. Then, like Flavius when he built his villa, they used flints and any other building material they could collect for the foundations, and wood and wattle and daub for the rest of the walls. Houses built of these materials soon fell into ruins and all that is left of them now may be a few little grass-covered mounds and banks or a scatter of flints.

If people happen to dig in places like these they may uncover pieces of Roman pottery or even the foundations of walls. Sometimes a burrowing rabbit will scrape out stones and pieces of pottery, or a big tree is blown down and then a passerby notices these things in the hole left by its roots. More often it is the

74

ploughman who sees them, especially if he ploughs for the first time a field which has always been kept for grass. Probably the farmer had already noticed that the grass in some parts of that field turned brown very quickly in a dry summer. This is because it was growing on top of the buried Roman walls and the roots could not get so much water. These dry patches may not seem to make any sort of pattern when seen from the ground, but if you look down on them from an aeroplane you sometimes see the walls of a building outlined very clearly. Then you can take an air photograph of them. Even if the walls lie a little way beneath the surface, too deep for the plough to touch, they may still be seen from the air in summertime because the crops growing on top of them will never be as tall and healthy as those with roots which can grow deeper down. Air photographs have shown us the whereabouts of many Roman camps, forts and villas. New discoveries like these are being made all the time.

3. *What we can learn from Roman buildings*

Of course this all depends on the kind of place it is. If we take a place like the villa at Lockleys, and dig down to its foundations very carefully, we find it had a long history. On top comes a small house with thin, roughly constructed walls built between A.D. 330 and 340. We will call it House No. 3. Probably people lived there until the end of the fourth century and then the building was deserted and gradually fell down. Underneath it lie the ruins of the much larger House No. 2 which was burnt down soon after the beginning of the fourth century. We can guess that the place then became deserted because the people who built House No. 3 obviously did not know it was there.

We already know a good deal about House No. 2 because it is the model for Flavius's villa. It was built soon after the middle of the second century and is really an enlargement of the smaller House No. 1 which lies underneath its corridor and some of its rooms (p. 61). House No. 1 was built between A.D. 60 and 70 and underneath it lie the huts in which some earlier first-century farmers probably lived.

75

You will have noticed how the word "underneath" keeps occurring in this description. All these different buildings lie one beneath another, the latest on top and the earliest at the bottom. So little is left of the earliest that it could easily have escaped notice altogether. The later builders might add on to the earlier house, they might alter only one part of it, or they might knock the whole thing down, clear away the ruins and build on top of them. It is very difficult for the archaeologist to find out which they did and he has to work very slowly and carefully, digging away the earth layer by layer. If he is lucky he will find pieces of pottery, coins, brooches and other small things which the people who lived there broke or lost. Everything he finds is carefully labelled and kept in separate boxes because we know that people used certain kinds of pottery in the second century and quite different kinds in the fourth. Fashions also changed in the brooches and other things they wore. The archaeologist looks through his finds to see if he has anything which will help him date his different layers. At the Lockleys villa he was fortunate, as the dates of Houses Nos. 1, 2 and 3 could all be discovered from the coins and the different sorts of pottery found there. Can you think why coins are so good for helping us fix the date of a house?

Uncovering a villa may tell us about life in one part of Britain during several hundred years. In the same way the archaeologist digs outside towns to try to find out the dates of their walls and defensive ditches, which probably changed at different periods. He tries to find out the history of buildings like the baths, Forum, and the temples inside the towns, and the headquarters, barracks and other buildings inside the forts. All the time he hopes to learn who built them, when they were built, and the sort of people who lived there.

4. *Latin, the Roman language*

The language which the Romans talked was Latin and we have taken many Latin words from them. For instance, the word 'province' comes from the Latin *provincia*, and 'colony' from the Latin *colonia*. The Latin for a dog is *canis*, and from this we get our word 'canine' which means 'dog-like'. Do you know which are your canine teeth? Do you think that this is a good word for them?

See how many words you can find in this book which you think come from Latin words. If you look them up in a big dictionary you will be able to see whether you are right.

Many of our place-names come indirectly from the Latin word *castra* which means a camp. When the Romans had left Britain, the people gradually forgot the Latin names by which the Romans called their towns. They only remembered where the Roman settlements had been and that the Latin name for them was something like *castra* or *ceaster* or *chester*. In this book you have visited Chester and Gloucester and Cirencester. What other English towns can you think of which end in this way? If you go to your local library and ask to see *The Oxford Dictionary of English Place-Names* you can look up all these places and find out more about how they came to be called by their present-day names. You will find, too, that the Welsh word *caer* means 'fort'. Can you think of some places in this book which are called 'fort'?

5. *How we can find out about Roman roads*

You may like to know more about Roman roads and how to look for them. Some of the most famous Roman roads are marked on the map on page 83. Several of our modern main roads are based on these roads. Perhaps you have travelled along them. In some places they exist nowadays only as lanes or as a ridge running across the countryside. Often they have been completely buried for many miles, and no one knows where they are. Then we have to hunt for clues on the air photographs, and in old books and maps which may show stretches of Roman roads before they were destroyed. Place names containing the word 'Street' or 'Strat' (e.g. Streatham or Stratford) are often connected with them.

The Romano-Britons had to keep the roads in order and sometimes when we dig a trench across a road we find traces of road repairs. On the next page is a picture of a section seen in the side of a trench dug across Dere Street near Corbridge. The earliest road was 35¾ feet wide, built up in several layers and edged with a kerb. It was repaired several times, the last time probably in the fourth century when the road was made narrower with a new kerb and a drain on either side.

Notice the different materials used to keep up this road. The original Dere Street had a hard gravel surface on top of a foundation of quarry stones over sand. But this, perhaps, was not strong enough, for it soon had to be repaired with more quarry stones; while cobbles were used for both the later surfaces.

Materials found locally such as gravel, stones and flints are the ones usually used in road-making, but at Holtye, near East Grinstead, Sussex, you can see part of a road built of slag from the nearby Roman iron workings. Occasionally stone paving was used, and a fine stretch of paved road exists between Rochdale and Halifax, at Blackstone Edge in Yorkshire. In some places a central rut has been worn in this road, probably by the brake-poles of the carts as they descended the hills.

II. WHAT WE CAN LEARN ABOUT ROMAN BRITAIN FROM THE REST OF THE ROMAN EMPIRE

When we think of Roman Britain we must always remember that Britannia was only one small province of the great Roman Empire. In the time of the Emperor Hadrian in the second century it reached from the borders of Persia and the Black Sea in the east, across Europe south of the River Danube to the Atlantic Ocean in the west, and from North Africa in the south to the mouth of the Rhine and the Scottish lowlands in the north. The Empire was ruled from Rome. Here is a map showing the Roman Empire at the time of the Emperor Hadrian.

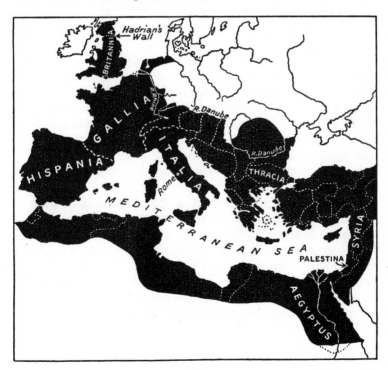

From Rome the government officials and the War Office made rules and gave orders which were very much the same for all the provinces. You can see the boundaries of the provinces marked on the map. Each one had a local governor who carried out the orders sent to him from the Emperor in Rome. Do you know what countries named on the map are called today?

Some of the rules and orders were written down and parts of them have survived until today. So we have the NOTITIA DIGNI-TATUM, a list of the civilian and army officials in different parts of the Empire and where they were stationed. We also have the ANTONINE ITINERARY, a road-book with a British section, giving routes for various journeys. These are very helpful to us. When we can learn very little from our inscriptions and excavations about what was happening in Britain, we can often use them to fill in the gaps by telling us what happened elsewhere. For instance, the legions used the same kind of weapons and built their forts with the same plans all over the Empire. So when we find forts in Africa which are much less ruined than our Roman forts, they help to give us a clearer picture of what forts in Britain were like. Fine sculptures in Rome show the army on parade and in battle, and our picture of soldiers making a temporary camp (page 21) comes from a great pillar, called Trajan's Column: it is carved all over with pictures of soldiers and battles.

So we can imagine our second-century Roman citizen, whether he was a Briton, a German or a Greek, free to travel anywhere he wished in the Empire without a passport. Wherever he went he would see things he knew—Roman roads, country villas, or towns with baths and temples. If he was a trader he had no difficulty over languages as he would always find people who understood Latin and used the same money and weights and measures as he had done all his life. The army fought and kept watch along the frontiers, there were few thieves and bandits along the roads, and everywhere he went he could travel in safety and peace.

THINGS TO DO

1. Dress some dolls like Gaius, Julius after his retirement, and Julia.

2. Explain some of the things the following people had to do in Roman Britain: *Centurion, legionary, standard bearer.*

3. Make up a conversation between Gaius and a National Service man today about life in the army.

4. What buildings would you expect to find inside a legionary fortress? Make a plan of them, and note what each was used for.

5. Write a description of a military parade and sports day that Gaius and Julius might have seen in the amphitheatre at Caerleon.

6. Make a model of part of Hadrian's Wall, including a mile-castle and a fort.

7. Life on Hadrian's Wall must sometimes have been very tedious. Imagine you are a friend of Gaius in the Second Legion, and write a letter to your family in Rome telling them what life on the Wall is like.

8. Would you rather have been a soldier or a civilian in Roman Britain?

9. Do you know any places where you can see Romano-British buildings? If you do, make a collection for your class of picture postcards and drawings of them.

10. In what ways did life in a Romano-British town resemble town life today?

11. Paint a picture of Julius working in his shop, with Victor helping him.

12. Make a list of the tools used by the Romano-Britons which are like those workmen use today. Perhaps your father has a plane or a chisel which you can compare with the pictures on page 67.

13. Make up the conversation in which Julius tells Flavius of his journey from Caerwent to Flavius's villa.

14. Paint a picture of the wagons being unloaded at the villa.

THINGS TO DO WITH THE MAP OF
ROMAN BRITAIN
(ORDNANCE SURVEY 1956 EDITION)

1. Look at the map and decide which way the men of the Second Legion probably went when they marched from Caerleon to near Housesteads, remembering that they stopped at Wroxeter (Viroconium) and Chester (Deva) on the way.

2. Are there any Romano-British sites marked near your home which you can visit?

3. When you go to London, Bath, Colchester or York, how many places do you pass which the map shows were also occupied in Roman times?

4. If you had been alive in Roman times which would have been your nearest town? Can you find out its Latin name?

5. Does your town or village lie near any Roman roads? Where do they lead to?

6. Ask your local library to let you see the large-scale Ordnance Survey of your district. See where the Roman roads go and try to follow them in the fields and lanes.

7. The large-scale maps will show where Romano-British things have been found and what they were. Make a map of your own showing them with different symbols like a little bowl for pottery, circles for coins, and little huts and houses for villages and towns. Put in the roads.

8. If there are only a few things to mark in, find out why. Was it because the soil was too poor to grow food, was the land probably covered with forest, or is it because no-one has bothered to look?

9. There are still lots of new discoveries to be found. If you live in the country watch when the farmer ploughs his fields and see if he has ploughed up any pieces of pottery.

10. If the map shows that you live in a Roman town or near Roman villas, look if there are any red tiles or pieces of carved stone or even Latin inscriptions built into the walls of any of the churches near you.

This map shows the main towns and roads in Roman Britain

THINGS TO DO IN MUSEUMS

1. Many towns have museums where you can see Romano-British discoveries. Find out which objects have been found near you and whether most of the things come from the town or the countryside.

2. Look at the pottery very carefully, particularly the red Samian, and then, when you see men digging deep trenches for drains or gas pipes or other work, or on new building sites, see if there are any bits of pottery lying on the heaps of soil. The red Samian looks so new that it is often thrown away because no-one knows that it is Roman. If you find any pieces of pottery, the museum will like to know about them: you should be able to tell them *exactly* where you found them.

3. See if there are any brooches, like the ones Julius made, in the museum.

4. Look at the portraits of the emperors on the Roman coins and see if you can find one of the Emperor Hadrian.

5. Find out if there are any inscriptions and what they mean.

6. The Romans worshipped other gods besides Jupiter, Mars and the others we have mentioned. Find out who they were and what sort of people they looked after in particular. You will often find their altars in the museums, and sometimes they are shown as bronze statuettes or on mosaic pavements. See if you can find out the names of any British gods like Cocidius and Coventina as well.

7. If you are ever in London, visit the Guildhall Museum at the Royal Exchange or the London Museum at Kensington Palace. There you will find many Roman tools and pots found in London that will remind you of the things we saw at Caerwent and Verulamium.

GLOSSARY

aisle: one of the two side passages in a building which is divided by pillars into three, a *nave* and two aisles.

amethyst: a violet-coloured precious stone.

amphitheatre: an oval or circular building having *tiers of seats* one above another around an open space, called the *arena*, and used for sports and shows.

amphora: a two-handled wine jar. (See illustration on page 9.)

ancestor: one from whom a person is descended, e.g. great-grand-father or great-great-grandmother.

anvil: the iron block upon which metals are shaped and hammered out by the smith.

apse: the semicircular bay sometimes found at one end of a temple or other building.

archaeologists: people who study the past, especially the periods before much history was written.

arena: see *amphitheatre.*

armourer: a man who either makes or looks after armour.

armoury: a place where armour is made or kept.

auxiliaries: soldiers conscripted from newly conquered tribes and sent to fight in other countries.

barracks: buildings where the soldiers live, especially in forts and fortresses.

basilica: in Roman times a large building used as meeting-place for business men and the *ordo* and as a law-court. Rather like our town halls.

book-scrolls: books written on long sheets of parchment or papyrus which were then rolled up.

boss: a large knob or stud.

capitals: the decorations at the top of a column.

capricorn: an imaginary animal, half goat and half fish.

centurion: the officer commanding a century.

century: see *legion*.

chaplet: a garland or wreath of flowers to be worn on the head.

charcoal: coal made by burning wood under turf or in some way which keeps out the air.

citizen: an inhabitant of a city. A Roman citizen was a free man or woman with certain rights and privileges and might be anyone whose parents were Roman citizens, not only the people who lived in Rome. The Roman citizenship could also be earned and the auxiliaries received it at the end of their twenty-five years' army service. (For a famous Roman citizen, see the story of St. Paul in *Acts* XXII. 25–29.)

cocoon: the covering grown by a caterpillar to protect itself while it turns into a butterfly.

cohort: see *legion*.

colonia: a town founded by the Roman government for retired legionaries. Each received a plot of land there as a gratuity.

colonnade: a row of columns placed at regular intervals.

coronet: an ornamental head-dress.

Cupid: the god of love shown as a small boy.

decurion: a member of the *ordo*.

denarii: Roman silver coins. The Romans used beautiful coins made of gold (the *aureus*), silver (the *denarius*), and bronze alloys (the *sestertius*, nearly as big as a penny, the *quadrans*, almost as big as a halfpenny, and the *as*, about the size of a farthing). The emperor's head appeared on one side, as the Queen's does today, and all sorts of things on the other, including portraits of other members of the Imperial family, the Emperor sacrificing at an altar or setting out on a journey, or pictures of gods or goddesses.

disc: a small circular object, more or less flat.

discus: the name of the top of a Roman lamp.

flint: a variety of quartz, greyish-black or yellowish in colour and used for building in parts of the country where there is no building stone.

flounce: a strip of material gathered round the skirt or hem of a dress like a frill.

flues: air passages along which travelled the smoke and fumes from the furnace.

fodder: food for animals.

Forum: the town square and market-place usually surrounded by shops and public buildings.

frontier: that part of a country which borders another country—in Roman Britain the limits of the area defended by the army.

garrison: a troop of soldiers stationed at a fortress or other place for defence.

girdle: a belt or band of material to tie round the waist.

gladiator: a man who fought in the *arena* of the *amphitheatre* for the amusement of the people.

granary: a store-house for grain.

gridiron: an iron frame placed over a fire on which food could be grilled.

hones: whetstones used for sharpening blades of scythes and other tools.

inscription: words cut or inscribed on a hard surface, usually of stone or metal.

javelin: a throwing spear.

knuckle-bones: small bones from the joints of animals.

ladle: a cup with a long handle used for dipping liquids out of a bowl or cauldron.

last: a wooden mould in the form of a human foot used by cobblers.

legate: the officer commanding a legion.

legion: a section of the Roman army, rather like a modern regiment. The legion was made up of ten *cohorts,* each usually of six *centuries.* In the second century A.D. there were eighty men in each century.

legionary: a soldier belonging to a legion.

looting: stealing.

lyre: a stringed instrument, a kind of harp.

magistrate: someone appointed to act as a judge, to sit in court and listen to complaints and quarrels, and to punish those who do wrong.

mason: a builder or worker in stone.

mortarium: a thick pottery bowl used for grinding and mixing food.

mosaic: a pavement made of a number of small stone cubes or *tesserae* of various colours arranged in different patterns.

municipium: an important native settlement recognized as a town by the Roman government.

nave: the middle of a building divided up by rows of columns—the space between the side corridors or aisles.

ordo: the town council. Its members, all retired magistrates, were called *decurions.*

palisade: a fence made of pieces of wood and used to defend a camp.

pedestal: the base upon which a statue stands.

pincers: tongs.

plane: a tool for smoothing wood.

quattuorviri: the four magistrates elected annually to preside over the *ordo* of a *municipium,* and look after all the town business.

quays: landing-stages where ships could anchor for loading and unloading.

rampart: earth banks or walls built to defend camps or forts. Sometimes they were stone walls, especially if they had a flat path protected by a breastwork built at the top. Along this sentries could walk and keep watch.

rhetor: teacher of the art of public speaking.

Romano-Briton: A Briton living in the Roman province of Britannia.

rubble: stones and bits of rock.

sapphires: a deep-blue precious stone.

scabbard: sheath for a sword or dagger.

scallop-shell: the shell of the shellfish called the scallop.

shaft: long handle.

shrine: a sacred place.

sickle: a knife curved in the form of a hook and chiefly used for cutting corn.

smithy: the blacksmith's workshop.

standard: a pole decorated in various ways with objects sacred to the Roman army and carried into battle by a soldier called the standard-bearer.

statuette: a very small statue.

stola: the long sleeveless dress worn by a Roman lady.

strigil: the curved implement used with oil for scraping the dust and perspiration off the bather in the hot room at the baths. Strigils are usually made of bronze, but bone and iron ones are sometimes found.

stylus: a small bronze or bone pointed tool used instead of a pen when writing on wax tablets.

surveyor: someone who measures land and makes plans for new roads and buildings.

tablets: thin pieces of wood covered with wax used for writing accounts and letters with a *stylus*.

tesserae: see *mosaic*.

thunderbolt: a shaft of lightning. The god Jupiter and the Roman eagle are often shown holding zig-zag pieces of metal which denote the thunderbolts they were believed to direct at mortals who annoyed them.

tiers of seats: rows of seats placed above each other. (See *amphitheatre*.)

tileries: places where tiles were made.

toga: the loose outer garment made of one long piece of cloth worn by Roman citizens.

tribunal: the place where the magistrate sat in the *Basilica*.

trident: a weapon with three prongs used by some gladiators, by fishermen as a fish spear, and also carried by Neptune.

tripod: a stand supported by three feet.

turf: a strip of grass dug up an inch or two deep so that the soil and roots cling together and make a little mat.

turnpike: a road with toll gates where travellers must stop and pay money for its upkeep.

turret: a small tower.

tusk: the long pointed tooth of animals like the boar or the elephant.

vallum: in Roman Britain the ditch which acted as a boundary to the military area just behind Hadrian's Wall.

venison: the flesh of deer.

veteran legionaries: old soldiers who have taken part in many battles or who have retired from the legion.

via principalis: the chief street passing right through a fort from one gate to the one in the opposite wall.

villa: in Roman Britain, a farm or country house.

wattle and daub: a method of building walls with osiers or reeds woven in and out of timber posts. The spaces between the reeds were filled in with mud or clay.

wheelwright: someone who makes wheels.